HAVE I GOT A CARTOON FOR YOU!

THE MOMENT MAGAZINE BOOK OF JEWISH CARTOONS

Edited with an Introd
BOB MAN
Former cartoon editor of *The New*

Foreword by
ROZ CHAST
Award-winning cartoonist and author

MomentBooks
Mandel Vilar Press

Copyright © 2019 by Cartoon Collections, LLC

All rights reserved. No portion of this book may be reproduced in any form or by any means, including electronic storage and retrieval systems, except by explicit prior written permission of the publisher. Brief passages may be excerpted for review and critical purposes.

This book is typeset in Gotham Book. The paper used in this book meets the minimum requirements of ANSI/NISO Z39.48-1992 (R1997). ∞

Cover illustration by Bob Mankoff
Design: Nadine Epstein & Anne Masters

Publisher's Cataloging-In-Publication Data

Names: Mankoff, Bob, compiler. | Chast, Roz, writer of supplementary textual content.
Title: Have I got a cartoon for you!: The Moment Magazine Book of Jewish Cartoons/Selected and introduced by Bob Mankoff; Foreword by Roz Chast.
Other Titles: Moment (New York, N.Y.)
Description: Washington, DC: MomentBooks; Simsbury, Connecticut: Mandel Vilar Press, [2019]
Identifiers: ISBN 9781942134596 (trade paperback)
Subjects: LCSH: Jews—Caricatures and cartoons. | Judaism—Caricatures and cartoons. | LCGFT: Cartoons (Humor)
Classification: LCC NC1763.J4 H38 2019 | DDC 741.53529924—dc23

Printed in the United States of America
19 20 21 22 23 24 25 26 27 / 9 8 7 6 5 4 3 2

MomentBooks
Moment Magazine, a division of the Center for Creative Change
4115 Wisconsin Avenue, NW, Suite LL10
Washington, DC 20016
momentmag.com/momentbooks
MomentBooks is a trade book imprint partner of Mandel Vilar Press

Mandel Vilar Press
19 Oxford Court, Simsbury, Connecticut 06070
americasforconservation.org | mvpublishers.org

FOREWORD
BY ROZ CHAST

Here are a few things about My People: we are fatalists. I.e., we tend to expect the worst. If you know anything about our history, you can see why we believe this. And when the worst does not happen, we don't celebrate our good fortune, because we know that it's just a matter of time before the flowerpot on the sixteenth floor falls off the windowsill and onto our head and kills us. My parents actually knew someone who was killed by a falling flowerpot. On the bright side, the widow sued the flowerpot owner, won, and bought a fancy apartment. If the dangers didn't come from windowsills, they'd come from within: gangrene; diphtheria, whooping cough; lockjaw; rabies; appendicitis; sudden blindness or deafness, mysterious "conditions," the disease that starts with C, a cold that turned into something, an infection that ended in amputation... If there were people who were joyful, or at least comfortable being alive, I did not live with them, and I did not know them. I don't think they lived in my neighborhood.

If there is a gene for anxiety, we have it bigtime. We ask a lot of questions, many of which are annoying. You can be an atheist or an agnostic and still be a Jew. We like to argue, because we are generally right. We do not feel shy about asking a waiter for another table because there's a draft, and also this chicken is raw. There's no such thing as chicken sushi, so please take it back.

Fighting with our fists is not usually our strong suit. If, or should I say WHEN, we are confronted by a galoot, words are our weapons of choice. Maybe not at the time—a galoot is often very large as well as very stupid—but later, in a cartoon. And yet, no matter how much contempt we have for a galoot, the self-deprecating joke is our true specialty. I.e., you can't insult me by calling me an unattractive, self-centered, no-talent nitwit, because (A) I already know that, and (B) I can hurt my feelings far, far better than you can. After all, I've had a lifetime of practice. To quote Larry David when he was questioned about being a self-hating Jew: "Let me tell you something. I do hate myself, but it has nothing to do with being Jewish."

Anxiety (how can a person not be anxious?!?), depression (ditto), aggression (passive or otherwise), the incessant need to question everything, a sense of the absurd, being interested in a wide range of subjects without knowing too much about any of them, knowing in your heart of hearts that you have always been and always will be an outsider, that you will never fit in no matter what you do or how "successful" you are, a combination of misanthropy and compassion for your fellow humans, and at least SOME ability to draw and write—this is what makes a cartoonist. This book is hilarious, and I hope you enjoy it as much as I do.

INTRODUCTION
BY BOB MANKOFF

Hi, I'm Bob Mankoff. I've been a cartoonist and cartoon editor at the *New Yorker* and now *Esquire* for over forty years, but I've been a Jew all my life, though not a religious one. I do observe Judaism, but from afar.

Look, I think the Old Testament is a decent first draft of how to behave. It's really a good try for 4,000 years ago, but we've come a long way since then, especially when it comes to laughs, which the Bible is not big on, at least not in a good way. God doesn't laugh with you; He laughs at you, with vehemence. If you say, "Stop me if you've heard this one," He will. For good.

> The kings of the earth stand ready, and the rulers conspire together against the Lord and his anointed king... The Lord who sits enthroned in heaven laughs them to scorn. *(Psalms 2:2–4)*

And it was not a very good idea to tease the Lord's messengers, the Hebrew prophets, as these tykes learned when they taunted Elisha:

He went up from there to Bethel and, as he was on his way, some small boys came out of the city and jeered at him, saying, "Get along with you, bald head, get along." He turned round and looked at them and he cursed them in the name of the lord; and two she-bears came out of a wood and mauled forty-two of them. *(2 Kings 2:23–24)*.

Bada bing, bada doom!

Needless to say, this book is not in the tradition of That Book. Not a she-bear to be found, although perhaps one is lurking out of sight, along of course, with a he-bear in the Noah's ark cartoon on page six. But rest assured they won't set upon you for enjoying the fun these cartoonists, Jew and non-Jew alike (our diversity panel demanded that), have with cartoon tropes about The People of The Book and the mores and mishugas of their neurotic diasporic descendants. Don't get me wrong. You don't have to be neurotic to be a member of the tribe, but hey, it doesn't hurt, even though, of course it does and has. But that head hurt, along with others, historic, millennia deep, and all too current, contributed to making the Jews more aptly called The People of The Joke rather than of The Book.

Humor feeds on contradiction, ambiguity, and absurdity. What could embody all those qualities better than the combination of Jewish chosenness and persecution? Hey, but on the upside we're funnier than anyone else, at least when it comes to being funny for money. In fact, a study done in 1979 found that four out of five people in professional comedy were Jewish. That said, next time, Lord, choose someone else.

For me as a kid in the late 1950s it could well have been five out of five. My parents would take me to the Catskills during the summer, to the Jewish resorts of Brown's Hotel, the Concorde, Grossinger's—the Borscht Belt—where I saw Jackie Mason (Yacov Maza) Buddy Hacket (Leonard Hacker), Rodney Dangerfield (Jacob Rodney Cohen), and Jerry Lewis (Joseph Levitch) do their shtick.

It wasn't called stand-up then. That term for a comedian wasn't in widespread use until the 1980s. Back then they were comedians, comics, and their kind of funny spritzing was pretty much a Jewish cottage industry or, since they were Jews, maybe a Jewish cottage cheese industry.

So how did we get from she-bears to shtick? Some scholars argue that Jewish humor stems from a method of studying the Talmud called *pilpul,* a kind of clever hairsplitting taken to hilarious extremes. An example:

> A baby pigeon that is found within fifty cubits of a pigeon coop is assumed to belong to the coop's owner. If it is found outside fifty cubits, then it belongs to whoever finds it. Rabbi Jeremiah asked: If one foot of the pigeon is within the fifty cubits and one foot is outside, who does the pigeon belong to? It was for this that they expelled Rabbi Jeremiah from the academy.

Leo Rosten describes *pilpul* as the "unproductive hairsplitting that is employed not so much to radiate clarity... as to display one's own cleverness." I go along with that except that I think the fine distinction making, logic chopping, and putting back together again, only to chop again, might result in a joke or a cartoon. Was I channeling the *pilpul* tradition when I wrote this *New Yorker* cartoon caption?

On Wall Street today, news of lower interest rates sent the stock market up, but then the expectation that these rates would be inflationary sent the market down, until the realization that lower rates might stimulate the sluggish economy pushed the market up, before it ultimately went down on fears that an overheated economy would lead to a reimposition of higher interest rates.

Or in this personal anecdote?

When we renovated our house, and my studio was finished, my wife said, "Now we can get rid of that green chair of yours." I said, "I don't want to get rid of it. It's where I read the paper. It's where I sit. I love my chair." She said, "If you like it so much, take it out to your new studio." To which I replied, "I don't want this ratty thing out there."

It's a bit of stretch but I do see what the philosopher Ludwig Wittgenstein would call a "family resemblance"—those things that share some combination of common, or related, qualities—rather than a rigorous single feature.

As a side note, Wittgenstein, who was Jewish, once said, "A serious and good philosophical work could be written consisting entirely of jokes." Now that's a philosophy I can get behind. A psychology I can back is in Sigmund Freud's *Jokes and Their Relation to the Unconscious,* published in 1905. It's both a serious psychological work and a great Jewish joke book. Here's are two classics from it:

The bridegroom was paying his first visit to the bride's house in the company of the broker, and while they were waiting in the salon for the family to appear, the broker drew attention to a cupboard with glass doors in which the finest set of silver plate was exhibited. "There! Look at that! You can see from these things how rich these people are." "But," asked the suspicious young man, "mightn't it be possible that these fine things were only collected for the occasion—that they were borrowed to give an impression of wealth?" "What an idea!" answered the broker protestingly. "Who do you think would lend anything to these people?"

The bridegroom was most disagreeably surprised when the bride was introduced to him, and drew the broker on one side and whispered his remonstrances: "Why have you brought me here?" he asked reproachfully. "She's ugly and old, she squints and has bad teeth and bleary eyes." "You needn't lower your voice," interrupted the broker, "she's deaf as well."

The insular world in which the topic of these jokes was relevant, Jewish matchmakers, is long gone, but these jokes are so perfectly formed that they will be told as long as jokes are told. It is this world— the world of primarily European Jewry in the last half of the nineteenth century— that is the source of the kind of humor that we, Jew, Gentile, and Whatever, enjoy and emulate in cartoon form in this book. As to whether they will have as long a life as those jokes, what can I say but L'Chaim!

HAVE I GOT A CARTOON FOR YOU!

"I love your early work."

EVE'S MOM

"No, you were right—this is much better than how it was before."

"Must I sacrifice family for career?"

"Wait for it."

"Where do you see yourself in forty years?"

"Yeah, I could walk all the way to Egypt. Or you
could just free them yourself using magic."

"Have your people let my people go."

"Was this in the forecast?"

"Thou shalt not create graven images, Ira. Thou shalt not take
the Lord's name in vain. Still looking at you, Ira. Thou shall keep
holy the Sabbath. You getting this, Ira?"

"He's all right. I just wish he were a little more pro-Israel."

"And here's a list of food you can't eat."

"A pillar of salt? Why, you poor, poor man."

"You may kiss the brides. You may kiss the concubines, but
don't make a big tzimmes about it."

"Go away. We're still Jewish."

"We got you a dreidel."

"Oh shoot, we still need to get Hanukkah gifts for the Rosenbaums."

"First of all, this conversation never happened."

"The Internet startup had only enough cash for one more day. But, miraculously, the money lasted for eight days, until more venture capital could be raised."

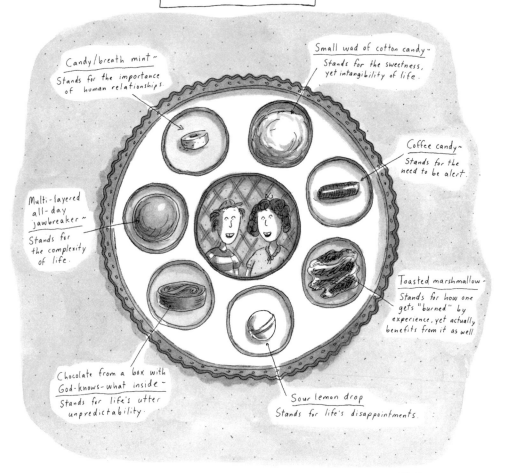

ALL-CANDY SEDER

Candy/breath mint~
Stands for the importance of human relationships.

Small wad of cotton candy~
Stands for the sweetness, yet intangibility of life.

Coffee candy~
Stands for the need to be alert.

Multi-layered all-day jawbreaker~
Stands for the complexity of life.

Toasted marshmallow~
Stands for how one gets "burned" by experience, yet actually benefits from it as well.

Chocolate from a box with God-knows-what inside~
Stands for life's utter unpredictability.

Sour lemon drop
Stands for life's disappointments.

R.Chst

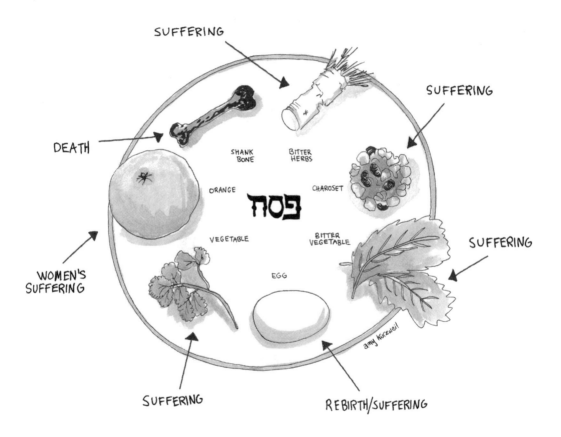

SEDER PLATE SYMBOLS EXPLAINED

SUFFERING

SUFFERING

DEATH

SHANK BONE

BITTER HERBS

CHAROSET

ORANGE

פסח

VEGETABLE

BITTER VEGETABLE

SUFFERING

WOMEN'S SUFFERING

EGG

amy kurzweil

SUFFERING

REBIRTH/SUFFERING

"Does dad know you're dating the guy from the Seder plate?"

"That was Elijah. He's stuck on the Garden State."

"The Kitmans in 12-B. Tell them Elijah is here for the Seder."

"...brisket... recipe. Hide it."

"That by you is a wish? 'A toasted bialy with cream cheese?'"

"Why is it we never focus on the things that unite us, like falafel?"

"You got maybe one that smells like cheese blintzes frying?

*"I'm sorry, sir, but you needed to order
the kosher meal when you were abducted."*

"What don't you understand? When my clients fly their guests
over your farm on the way to Vegas, they'd like to see
the words 'Mazel tov, Josh' spelled out in your cornfield."

SHOTGUN BAR MITZVAH

Kanin

"And I'm telling you this, young man—if you join the Children's Crusade, you needn't expect any presents at your bar mitzvah."

"Open the pod bay doors, HAL—we can't wait for the Shabbos goy."

"Why are you arguing?"   "I'm not arguing. I'm Jewish."

"I'm Jewish and Don is Catholic, but we're raising the kids as wolves."

JEWS FOR JESUS AND ALSO FOR PISSING OFF ONE'S PARENTS, EVEN IF THEY WEREN'T RELIGIOUS, IN A WAY THAT THE HARE KRISHNAS CAN'T EVEN **BEGIN** TO IMAGINE.

"No, we're not Jewish, but we think it would be fun for our reception's theme to be 'A Jewish Wedding'."

"Look, darling, he's your baby and you can name him what you want, but Mohammed Ginsburg?"

"It's a litte ungapatchka, don't you think?"

"I forgot my wig."

"And remember, if you need anything I'm available 24/6."

"Too Jewish?"

"We're sitting shiva for Oren. He lost his Air Pods."

"I'm not beached. I just don't swim on Saturdays."

AT THE AGE OF 39, SIDNEY SUSSMAN BECAME UNDENIABLY AWARE OF HIS JEWISHNESS

"This will never work, David. Your family is significantly
less non-observant than mine."

ARCHEOLOGISTS DISCOVER EVIDENCE THAT EARLY CAVEMEN WERE JEWISH
YOU'RE RIGHT! IT IS A MEZUZAH!

"And just why is this knight different from all other knights?"

SLALOM

sdf

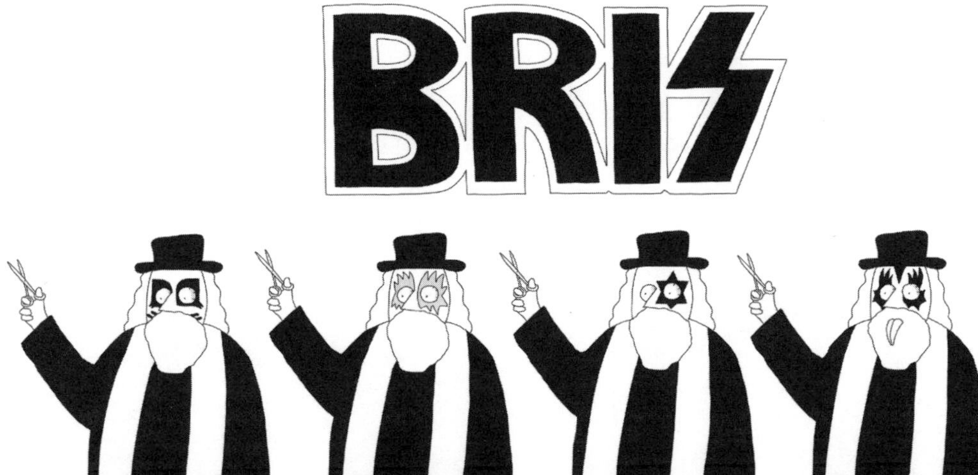
BRIS
sdf

"I do hope you're here for the circumcision."

"Kvetch dirty to me, honey."

"Pishers and kvetchers, reporting for duty."

"Kfetch!"

"I had that, only worse."

"Any other hobbies besides suffering?"

"Einstein, Szilard, Teller, Openheimer..
but you look through the Old Testament and through the Talmud,
and there's not a _word_ about Physics."

"Yes, I do prefer the mission... that is, the Rabbinic posiiton."

STREET BUBBES

At Bubbe's Condo

"Third marriage."

MY FATHER'S FAVORITE YIDDISH JOKE

Herschel was going on a date. He was very nervous, because he didn't have a lot of experience in that area.

He decides to consult his friend Sid — the "playboy."

Vot are we going to talk about?!?...

Sid tells him:

Just remember the three F's: Food, Family, and Filosophy — and you can't go wrong!

Finally comes the date.

So! Do you hev a bruddeh?

No.

TICK TOCK TICK TOCK

FIVE MINUTES PASS

TICK TOCK

Do you like honeycake?

No.

TICK TOCK

ANOTHER FIVE MINUTES PASS

TICK TO

If you had a bruddeh, would **he** like honeycake?

r.Chs

YENTA THEATRE PRESENTS:
WAITING FOR GODOT
So, where's Godot?
He's always late.
Maybe something happened to him!!!
I heard he moved to Florida.
R. Chst

"...then click 'save settings', scroll down to 'done' and voila! You're Facebook
stalking Miriam's daughter's new husband."

"I still want grandchildren."

"Deploy countermeasures, for crying out loud! Oy, you're just like your father but lazier."

"That's the Statue of Do What Your Mother Tells You."

"Twenty-thousand eggs, but do they ever call?"

THE MOTHER OF DAMOCLES

"In order to get the most accurate stress test results, we're going to have your mother administer it."

ARTISTS

Me a few years ago.

All the cartoons in this book are available for licensing
on cartooncollections.com.